CW00689727

Published by: Cross Media Ltd.
13 Berners Street, London W1T 3LH, UK
Tel: 020-7436-1960   Fax: 020-7436-1930

Project Manager: Kazuhiro Marumo
Editor: J.L.Rollinson
Designer: Misa Watanabe
Photographer: Naomi Igawa, Hiroshi Mitani
Recipes: Nobuko Motohashi
Chef: Miyoko Yoshimura (Akasha Cooking School)
Coordinator: Masahiko Goto. Thanks to: Akasha Tokodo & Sono Aoki

ISBN 1-897701-72-1
Printed in Japan

All about rice

The staple food that keeps you in good health

Rice farming dates back some 7,000 years and began in China. As methods of productivity improved, farmers were able to make more effective planning for increasing the yield and rice farming gradually spread to other parts of the world from Southern China and South East Asia. The Japanese began cultivating rice from 300AD and it soon became their staple food. The particular carbohydrate in rice makes up 76% of its nutritional value. It is easy to digest, converts to energy very rapidly, and this energy is long lasting.

In terms of calorific value, 100g of bread provides 260kcal, whereas 100g of rice provides a mere 148kcal, as rice is digested rather more slowly. This means that the amount of insulin secreted is small, making it harder to convert into fat. The fact that rice is less easily converted into fat suggests that it is an appropriate food for people who are diabetic or who are concerned about their weight.

How to cook rice

[How to wash rice]

The secret of cooking good rice is to wash it with care.

Measure the rice accurately and pour a generous amount of water over it. Stir it swiftly with one hand and discard the water immediately. Stir the rice thoroughly with the tips of the fingers, add more water, mix, and discard the water again. Repeat this procedure 4-5 times until the water runs clear then drain well in a sieve.

[How to use a rice cooker]

The easiest way to cook rice

1   Place the washed rice in a rice cooker and pour water up to the necessary mark, and switch the cooker on.

[How to cook rice using a pan]
It is best to use a heavy-based pan

First, wash the rice in the prescribed way. When you cook the rice in a pan, it is important to use a heavy-based pan as this makes it less likely to boil over, allowing the rice to simmer well.

1 Place the washed rice and the water (the proportion of rice to water is 200ml-220ml water to 150g rice) in a heavy-based pan, put the lid on and bring it to the boil. When the lid starts to clatter, wait for 15-20 seconds and then lower the heat.

2 Leave the rice to cook on a low heat for 13-15 minutes, and raise the heat just before cooking is complete. Leave the pan covered for 10 minutes. Remove the lid and if the grains on the surface have risen slightly, the rice has been nicely cooked.

Types of rice

Long grain, short grain

White rice comes in two main varieties, the long grain *Indica* rice and the short grain *Japonica* rice. Indica rice forms 80% of the world's rice production, is less glutinous than the Japonica and suitable for cooking dishes such as pilafs, curries, and fried rice. Japonica rice is the staple food of countries such as Japan, China and large areas of Asia. Japonica rice production makes up less than 15% of the world's rice production. It is characterised by its rich taste and glutinous texture.

Other varieties of rice include brown rice, which is unpolished, making it a richer source of vitamins, minerals and protein, and the most glutinous Japanese rice variety which consists of 100% amylopectin starch and is used for making rice cakes or Japanese sweets.

Indica rice   Japonica rice   brown rice   glutinous Japanese rice

How to store rice

How to store rice

Keep the rice in an airtight container. Uncooked rice can be stored in the fridge or in a well-ventilated place that avoids sunlight. Rice has no sell-by date, but whilst it doesn't become unsafe to consume, it will deteriorate in quality the longer it is kept. As a guideline, rice polished during the summer is best eaten within two weeks. Rice polished at any other time of year, is best consumed within a month.

How to store cooked rice (white rice)

When you have some spare cooked white rice, wrap it up in clingfilm in small quantities and freeze it. Defrost it in a microwave or steamer. When re-heating the rice, a splash of *sake* (Japanese rice wine) will remove the unpleasant smell which occurs when cooked rice has been frozen and defrosted. Cooked rice can be kept in the freezer for a month.

Rice with Chicken and Vegetables

● 五目炊き込み御飯　*Gomoku Takikomi-gohan*　●

Serves 4

450g rice
½ carrot
100g burdock root
100g *shiitake*
60g chicken breast
20g fried bean curd
　(1 block)

[A]
660ml soup stock
3 tbsps soy sauce
1 tbsp *sake*
1 tbsp *mirin*

* See page 4 how to wash the rice

1　Cut the carrot into strips, 3cm x 2mm. Peel the burdock root and cut it into shavings, soak it in water to soften. Remove the stems of the *shiitake* and cut them into strips (5mm).

2　Cut the chicken into bite size pieces, and the bean curd into blocks, 4-5cm x 1cm.

3

Place the rice, vegetables, chicken and bean curd into a rice cooker with A. Mix lightly and cook (if using a pan follow the directions on page 5).

Rice and Chestnuts

栗ご飯 *Kuri-gohan*

Serves 4

450g rice
12-16 chestnuts
black sesame seeds,
toasted (to garnish)

[A]
660ml soup stock
1 tbsp *sake*
1 tbsp *mirin*
1 tsp salt

* See page 4 how to wash the rice

1. Shell the chestnuts, removing any skin.

2. Soak chestnuts in water for 2-3 hours, then cut the larger ones into several pieces.

3. Place the rice, chestnuts, and A in a rice cooker. Mix lightly and cook (if using a pan follow the directions on page 5).

4. Serve it in a bowl and sprinkle with toasted black sesame seeds.

Rice and Mushrooms

● きのこご飯 *Kinoko-gohan* ●

450g rice

100g each:
shimeji mushrooms,
enoki mushrooms,
shiitake mushrooms

600ml soup stock

3 tbsps soy sauce

1 tbsp *sake*

1 tbsp *mirin*

* See page 4 how to wash the rice

1 Remove the firm stems and mycelium of the *shimeji* and *enoki*, cut the *enoki* in half. Remove the stems of the *shiitake*, cut into fine strips (5mm wide) and rinse all the mushrooms.

2

Place the rice, mushrooms, soup stock, soy sauce, *sake*, and *mirin* in a rice cooker. Mix lightly and cook (if using a pan follow the directions on page 5).

Rice and Peas

● 豆ご飯 *Mame-gohan* ●

* See page 4 how to wash the rice

Serves 4

450g rice
225g fresh peas
660ml soup stock
1½ tbsp *sake*
2 tsp *mirin*
¼ tsp salt

1 Shell peas.

2 Place rice, soup stock, *sake*, *mirin* and salt into a rice cooker.

3

Add the peas and spread them evenly over the top of the rice, and cook (if using a pan follow the directions on page 5).

Chicken with Egg Bowl
● 親子丼 *Oyako-don* ●

Serves 1

130g rice

50g chicken thigh

¼ leek

1 egg

75ml soup stock

20ml soy sauce

20ml *mirin*

some dried seaweed
and chervil
(to garnish)

* See page 4 how to wash the rice
* See page 4 how to cook the rice

1 Cut the chicken into bite size pieces. Cut the leek diagonally into thin slices. Place the chicken, leek, soup stock, soy sauce and *mirin* in a frying pan and bring to the boil.

2 Pour the beaten egg over the top of the ingredients to cover the surface. When it starts to boil again, turn off the heat and leave it to settle for 1-2 minutes.

3 Place the chicken and egg topping carefully over the rice. and garnish with chopped seaweed and chervil.

Pork Cutlet Bowl

● カツ丼 *Katsu-don* ●

This dish is rich in B vitamins.

* See page 4 how to wash the rice
* See page 4 how to cook the rice

Serves 1

130g rice
1 pork loin chop
¼ medium size onion
1 egg
some vegetable
or sunflower oil
for deep-frying

1 Make 4-5 cuts along the chop, being careful not to cut right through. Season it with salt and pepper. Coat thinly with flour, dip it into the beaten egg, and then coat it with the breadcrumbs.

Katsu-don

. . . .

[breadcrumb coating]

a handful of plain flour

1 egg, lightly beaten

a handful of breadcrumbs

[sauce]

75ml soup stock

20ml soy sauce

20ml *mirin*

1 tbsp *sake*

2 Heat some oil in a deep frying pan. Deep-fry the pork until it floats on the surface of the oil.

3 Place the pork on kitchen paper to remove excess oil. Cut it into bite size pieces.

4 Cut the onion into thin slices.

Tip!

To keep the egg soft and fluffy, don't cook it too long once it's added to the pan.

5 Place the pork, onions, and the sauce in a frying pan, bring to the boil, then lower the heat and simmer for 2-3 minutes.

 Pour the beaten egg in evenly to cover the surface, cover with a lid, and cook for 1 minute on a lower heat.

7 The pork and sauce are then served up on a bowl of rice.

Beef Bowl

● 牛丼 *Gyū-don* ●

* See page 4 how to wash the rice
* See page 4 how to cook the rice

Serves 1

130g rice
100g thinly sliced beef
1/4 onion
1/2 tbsp vegetable or sunflower oil
some red pickled ginger

[A]
240ml soup stock
1 tbsp soy sauce
1 tbsp *mirin*
1 tbsp *sake*
1 tbsp sugar

1 Cut the onion into slices (5mm). Cut the beef into bite size pieces (3cm).

2  Heat the oil in a pan and fry the onion and the beef. Add A, bring it to the boil, and then lower the heat and cook for 10 minutes. Skim off any scum whilst it cooks.

3 Place the rice in a bowl, and pour over the cooked topping. Garnish with red pickled ginger.

22

Tempura Bowl

● 天丼 *Ten-don* ●

This dish originally dates back to the 16th century.

Serves 1

Serves 1

130g rice

2 shrimps

1 aubergine

4 green beans

some vegetable
or sunflower oil
for deep-frying

* See page 4 how to wash the rice
* See page 4 how to cook the rice

1 Shell and devein the shrimps.
Cut off the tips of the shrimp
tails, then score the undersides
several times.

24

[batter]
100g plain flour, sifted
1 egg
160ml cold water

[sauce]
50ml soup stock
15ml soy sauce
15ml *mirin*

2 Use the aubergine whole if they are very small, otherwise cut them in slices.

3 Cut the beans in half.

4 To make the batter, beat the egg in a bowl, add the cold water and flour, and mix lightly.

5 Heat the oil in a heavy-based deep pan.

6 Dip the shrimps, aubergine, and beans into the batter and deep-fry them until they float on the surface of the oil. Place them on kitchen paper to remove excess oil.

7 Place all the sauce ingredients in a small pan and bring them to a boil. Arrange the *tempura* on a bowl of rice and pour the sauce over.

Minced Raw Tuna Bowl

ねぎとろ丼 *Negitoro-don*

* See page 4 how to wash the rice
* See page 4 how to cook the rice

Serves 1

130g rice

75g fresh tuna
(lean, minced)

¼ spring onion

¼ sheet
dried seaweed
(10.5cm × 9.5cm)

some soy sauce

some wasabi

1 Chop the spring onion into
fine slices (2mm), and the
dried seaweed into fine strips.
Mince the tuna.

2

Place the rice in a bowl and
spread the raw tuna on top.
Sprinkle the spring onion
and the seaweed over the
dish and garnish with *wasabi*.
Before eating, add some soy
sauce.

Savoury Sticky Rice

おこわ *Okowa*

An ideal dish for anyone on a diet as it stems that hungry feeling.

Serves 4

450g glutinous rice

70g chicken thigh

70g boiled bamboo shoots

3 *shiitake* mushrooms

40g carrots

20g fried bean curd (1 block)

* See page 4 how to wash the rice

1 Cut the chicken, bamboo shoots, carrots, bean curd and *shiitake* into fine strips (5mm wide), and mix them with A in a bowl.

Okowa

. . . .

[A]
3 tbsps soy sauce
1 tsp sugar
1 tsp *mirin*

[B]
100ml soup stock
50ml *sake*

2 Mix them with the rice and place them in a steamer (following the method on page 32). Steam the ingredients on high for 20 minutes.

3 Remove them from the steamer and put them in a bowl. Mix well with B.

4 Place all the ingredients in the steamer and steam for a further 20 minutes.

Okowa

Tip!

Add a drop more boiling water when it evaporates.

[How to steam glutinous rice]

1 Boil ¾ of a pan of water.

2 Spread a muslin cloth carefully over a steamer. Spread the rice evenly on the cloth, and make a shallow hollow in the centre of the rice.

3 Place the steamer on top of the pan, steam it on high for 40 minutes. Pinch a grain and if it squashes easily the rice is ready.

Red Rice with Azuki Beans

赤飯 *Seki-han*

* See page 4 how to wash the rice

Serves 4

450g glutinous rice
50g *azuki* beans
1 litre water
a pinch of
black sesame and salt

1 Wash *azuki* beans, boil for 5-6 minutes then discard the water. Add 500ml of fresh water to the pan of beans over the heat. When it comes to the boil, turn it down low, and cook the beans until tender. Drain in a sieve, reserving the hot water in a bowl and allowing it to cool.

2

Soak the rice in the cool bean water for 1-2 hours, so that the rice soaks up the colour of the *azuki* beans. Drain the rice once it has coloured.

3 Mix the rice with the *azuki* beans. Place them in a steamer and steam for 40 minutes, (following the method on page 32). Serve the rice sprinkled with sesame and salt.

Rice Ball

おにぎり *Onigiri*

* See page 4 how to wash the rice
* See page 4 how to cook the rice

Makes 1

80g rice

1/8 sheet
dried seaweed
(cut a standard size
sheet down to
5.25cm × 9.5cm
for each rice ball)

some salt

[filling]

grilled, shredded
salted salmon,
pickled plums,
salted cod roe
or tuna

1 Wet the palms of your hands and then lightly rub them with salt. Spread the rice in the palm of one hand, making a small hollow for the filling in the centre.

2 Shape the rice into a triangular form with the rice enclosing the filling.

3 Wrap the dried seaweed around the shaped rice ball.

Tea and Rice (salmon)

● お茶漬け *Ocha-zuke* ●

So-called because the stock can be replaced by green tea

* See page 4 how to wash the rice
* See page 4 how to cook the rice

Serves 1

130g rice

30g salmon

¼ sheet
dried seaweed
(10.5cm × 9.5cm)

300ml soup stock

2ml soy sauce

a pinch of salt

½ tsp *wasabi*

1 Rub the salmon lightly with salt, grill it and then slice it into fine strips. Crumple the dried seaweed lightly by hand and cut it into fine strips.

2 Place the soup stock, soy sauce, and salt in a saucepan and heat it through.

3  Serve the rice in a bowl, laying the salmon on top and pouring the heated stock over it. Sprinkle with dried seaweed and garnish with *wasabi*. Stir lightly before eating.

Rice Porridge

● おかゆ *Okayu* ●

* See page 4 how to wash the rice

Serves 1

75g rice
500ml water
pinch of salt

1 Place the washed rice and water in a pan without a lid, bring it to the boil then lower the heat and cook for 5-6 minutes.

2 Lower the heat further and cook for another 20-25 minutes.

3

Just before it has finished cooking, add a little salt and cover with a lid, turn off the heat and leave it for 5 minutes.

Fried Rice

チャーハン　*Chā-han* ●

* See page 4 how to wash the rice
* See page 4 how to cook the rice

Serves 2

160g-240g rice

2 eggs (beaten)

2 tbsps chopped leek

1 ½ tbsp vegetable or sunflower oil

some salt & pepper

1 ½ tsp *sake*

1 Heat the oil in a wok. Pour in the beaten eggs and scramble them. Remove from heat and set aside.

2 Add some more oil and fry the rice on high. Add the eggs and the chopped leek, stir-fry taking care that the rice does not stick together.

3 Season with salt, pepper and *sake*.

Rice Omelette

オムライス *Omu-raisu*

The Japanese omelette

* See page 4 how to wash the rice
* See page 4 how to cook the rice

Serves 1

130g rice

2 eggs

$\frac{1}{6}$ onion

30g chicken breast

1-2 tbsps
tomato ketchup
(for seasoning)

1 $\frac{1}{2}$ tsp butter

1 Chop the onion; cut the chicken into 1cm cubes and season with salt and pepper.

some salt and pepper

some vegetable
or sunflower oil

some tomato ketchup
(to garnish)

2 Swirl the butter in a frying pan and fry the chicken and onion.

3 When cooked, add the rice and stir-fry them, mixing the ingredients well.

4 Season with salt, pepper, and tomato ketchup (adjust according to taste).

45

Tip!

Don't mix the ketchup into the rice too well or it becomes too sticky.

5 Heat the oil in another frying pan. Pour in well-beaten eggs seasoned with salt and pepper. When the eggs are almost cooked (not dry), place the fried rice on top, folding the omelette around the rice.

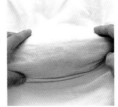

Shape the omelette. Serve on a plate with tomato ketchup.

• Guide to ingredients - Rice •

Abura-age	—	fried bean curd – 1 block refers to 20g (fried tofu)
Azuki	—	small red beans
Benishoga	—	red pickled ginger
Dashi	—	Japanese soup stock
Enoki	—	very thin white mushrooms
Gobo	—	burdock root
Mirin	—	cooking sake (sweet)
Mitsuba	—	chervil
Mochigome	—	Japanese glutinous rice (short grain rice)
Nori	—	sheet of dried seaweed – 'standard size' refers to sheet: 21cm x 19 cm
Sake	—	Japanese rice wine
Shiitake	—	variety of mushroom
Shimeji	—	small brown-topped mushrooms
Takenoko	—	bamboo shoots
Umeboshi	—	Japanese pickled plums
Wasabi	—	Japanese horesradish